Dear Daddy,

This coupon book is m
for your hard work, patience, and love. Whenever
you need to, just hand the coupon back to me
(you may have to read it for me, too!) and I will be
happy to do whatever the coupon says. You can
use the back of each coupon to record the date
and any special feelings we shared that day!

Dear Daddy Coupons

Sourcebooks
Naperville, IL

Copyright © 1999 by Sourcebooks, Inc.
Cover and internal design by Eric O'Malley, Sourcebooks, Inc.

Published by Sourcebooks, Inc.   P.O. Box 372, Naperville, IL 60566   630.961.3900
Fax: 630.961.2168

ISBN: 1-57071-451-7

Printed and bound in the United States of America
10 9 8 7 6 5 4 3 2 1

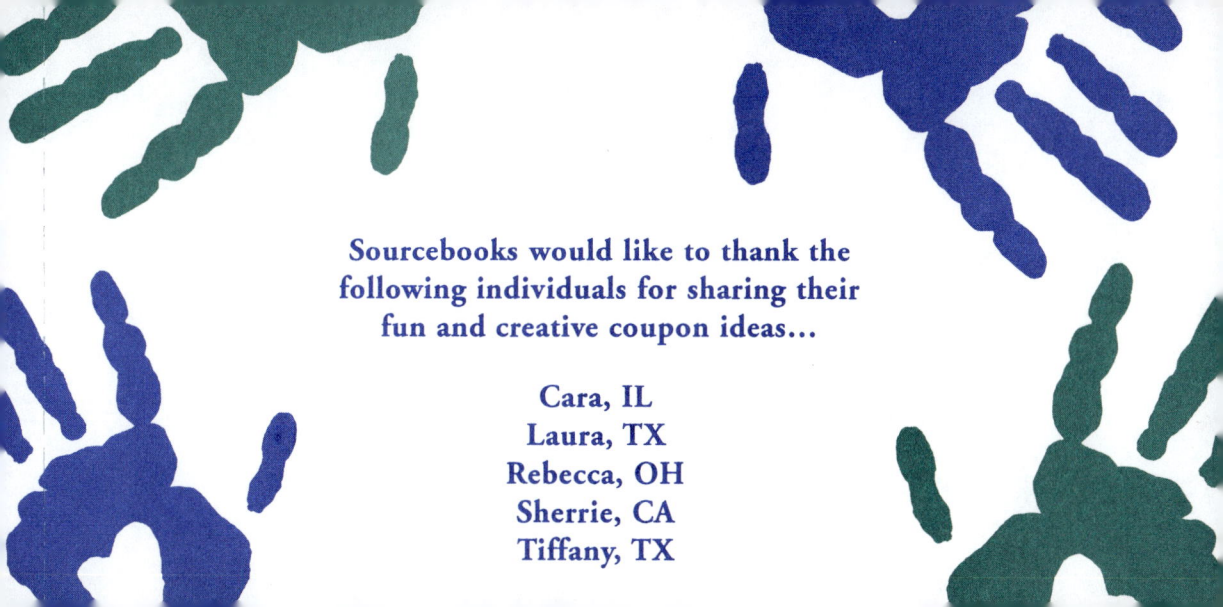

Sourcebooks would like to thank the
following individuals for sharing their
fun and creative coupon ideas...

Cara, IL
Laura, TX
Rebecca, OH
Sherrie, CA
Tiffany, TX

Dear Daddy,
I will give you
an honest answer.

Date:

Special Feelings:

Dear Daddy,
I promise to
practice my very
best manners.

Date:

Special Feelings:

Dear Daddy, This coupon lets you watch the movie of your choice in peace.

Date:

Special Feelings:

Dear Daddy,
I will give you
a foot massage.

Date:

Special Feelings:

Dear Daddy,
I will let you give
me a piggy back
ride today.

Date:

Special Feelings:

Dear Daddy, I promise
to giggle at your jokes—
even the ones
I've heard before.

Date:

Special Feelings:

Dear Daddy,
I will help you
with your chores.

Date:

Special Feelings:

Dear Daddy,
I promise not
to jump on my
bed—or yours!

Date:

Special Feelings:

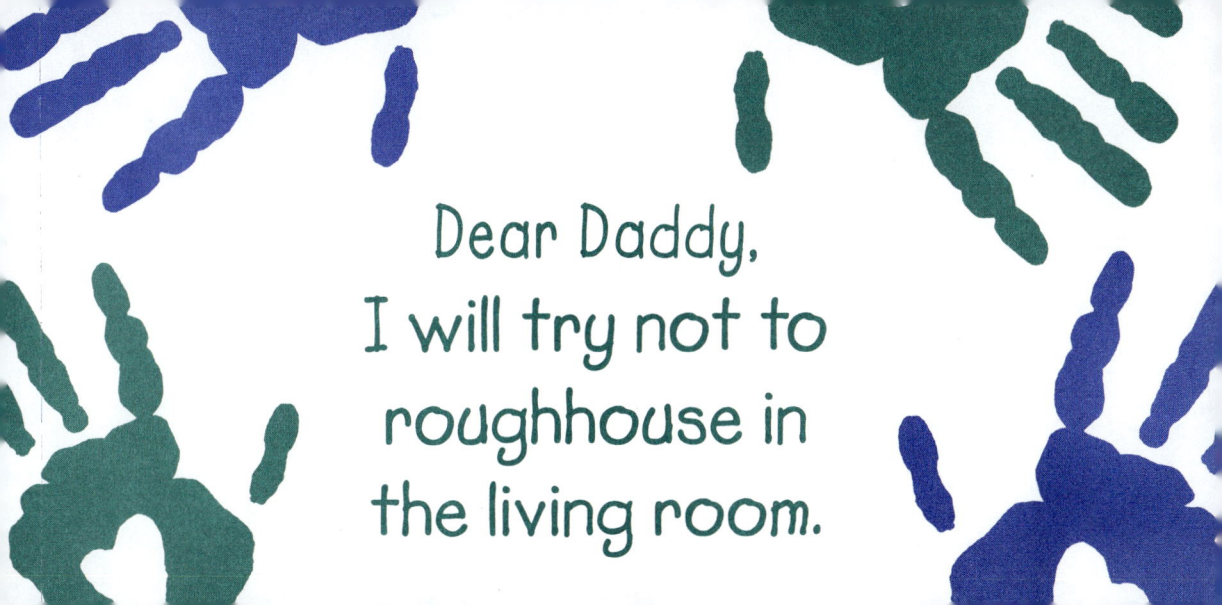

Dear Daddy,
I will try not to
roughhouse in
the living room.

Date:

Special Feelings:

Dear Daddy,
Today I'll let
you win a board
game for once.

Date:

Special Feelings:

Dear Daddy,
I will give you
one hour of quiet
time this afternoon.

Date:

Special Feelings:

Date:

Special Feelings:

Dear Daddy,
I will let you
hold the remote
control tonight.

Date:

Special Feelings:

Dear Daddy,
I will not leave my
toys on the stairs
or in the hallway.

Date:

Special Feelings:

Dear Daddy,
This coupon entitles
you to one free
backscratch.

Date:

Special Feelings:

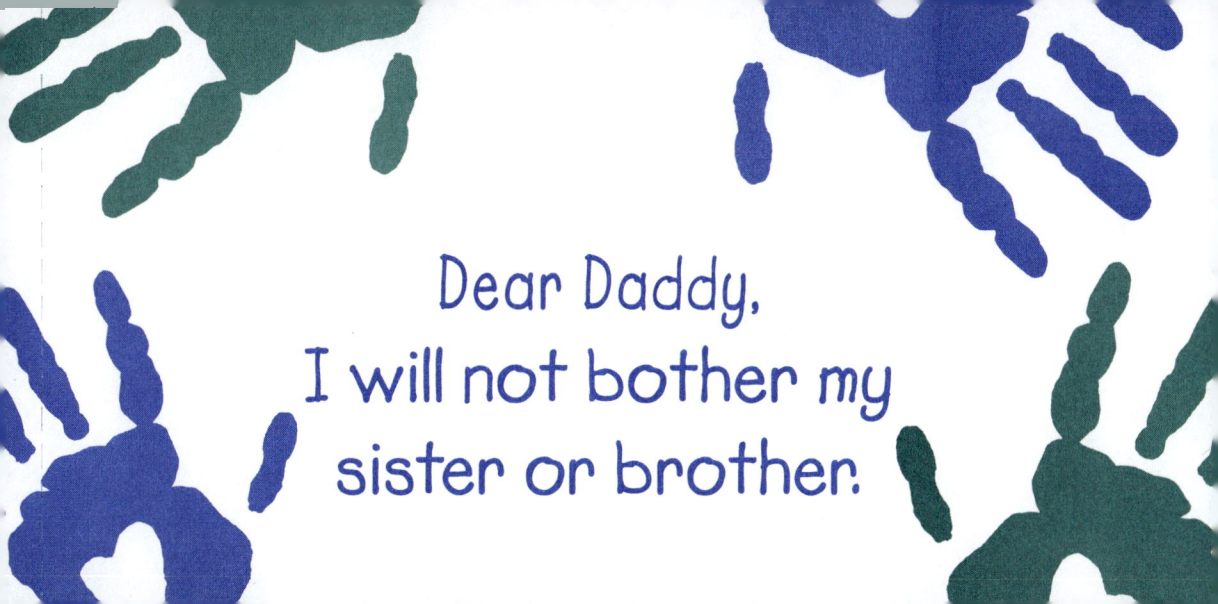

Dear Daddy,
I will not bother my
sister or brother.

Date:

Special Feelings:

Dear Daddy,
I will stay in bed
once the lights
are turned off.

Date:

Special Feelings:

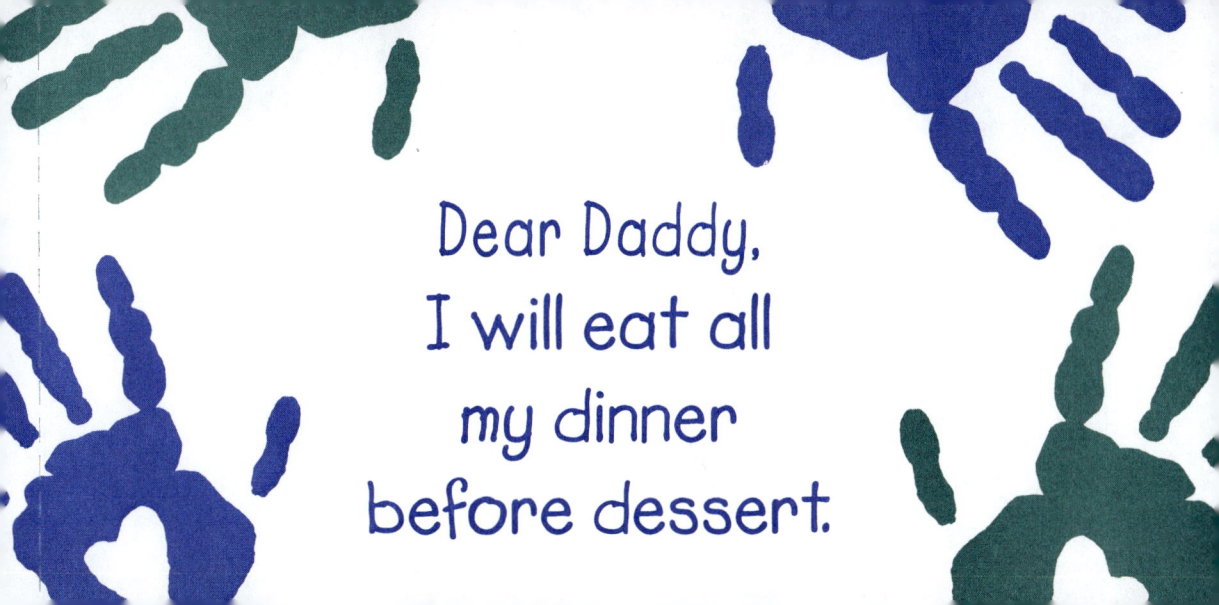

Dear Daddy,
I will eat all
my dinner
before dessert.

Date:

Special Feelings:

Dear Daddy,
I will play quietly
by myself while
you make dinner.

Date:

Special Feelings:

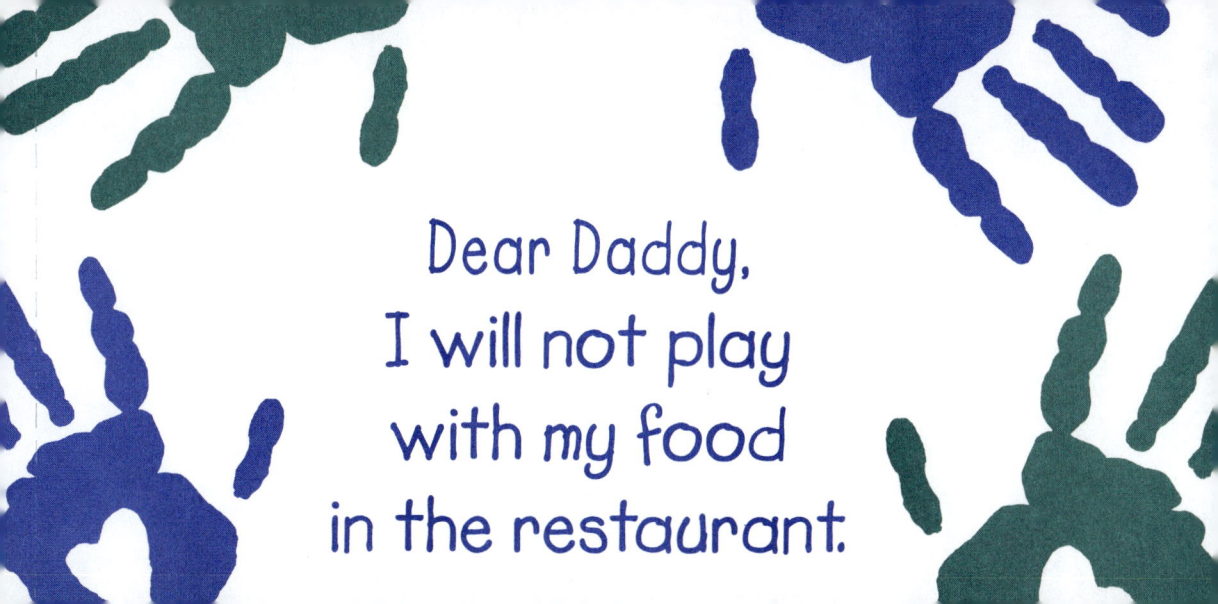

Dear Daddy,
I will not play
with my food
in the restaurant.

Date:

Special Feelings:

Dear Daddy,
I will tell
you a joke.

Date:

Special Feelings:

Dear Daddy,
I will let you
enjoy a lazy
Saturday morning.

Date:

Special Feelings:

Dear Daddy, I will share hot chocolate with you on a cold night.

Date:

Special Feelings:

Dear Daddy,
Tonight I'll read
you a story
at my bedtime.

Date:

Special Feelings:

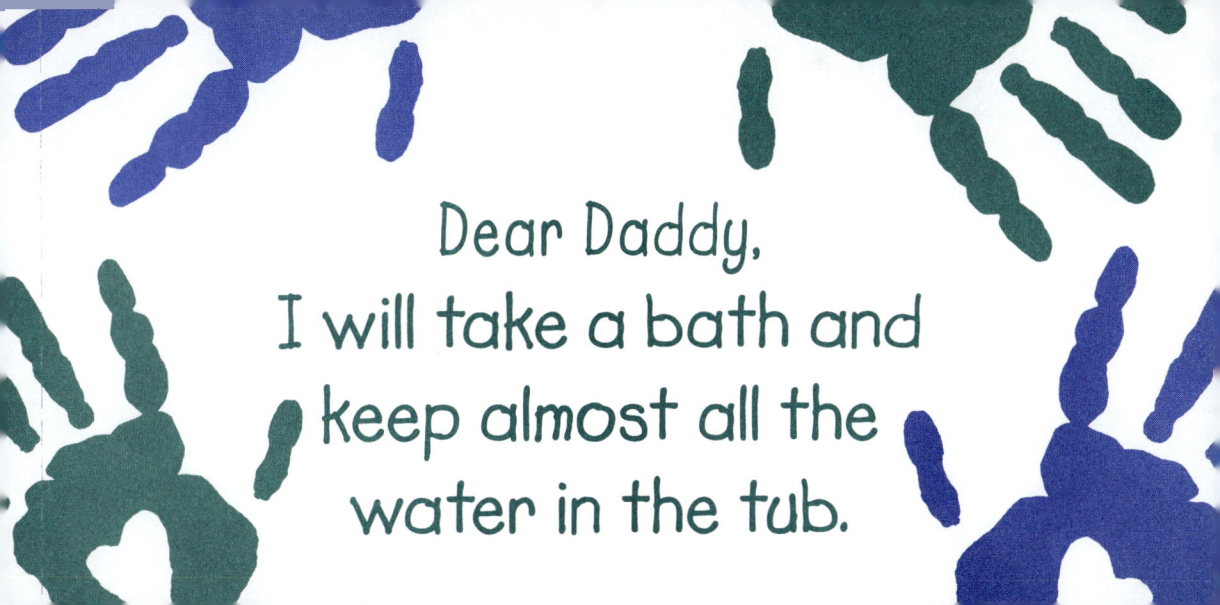

Dear Daddy,
I will take a bath and keep almost all the water in the tub.

Date:

Special Feelings:

Dear Daddy,
This coupon is
good for 10 hugs
in one day.

Date:

Special Feelings:

Dear Daddy,
I will turn
the TV off.

Date:

Special Feelings:

Dear Daddy,
I will share
my teddy bear
with you.

Date:

Special Feelings:

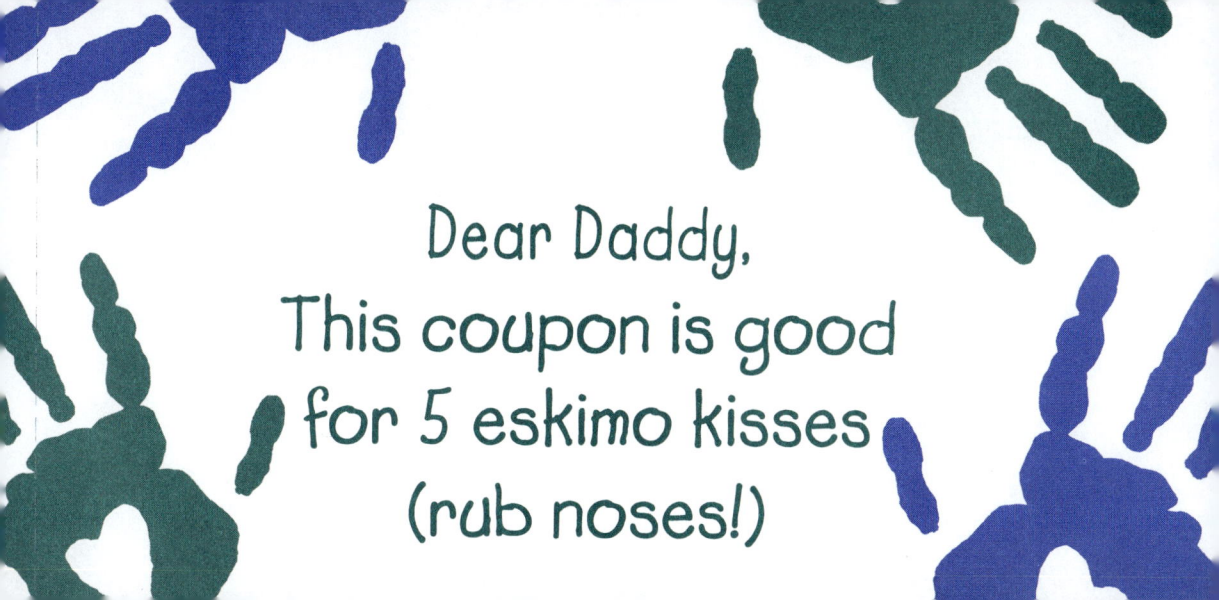

Dear Daddy,
This coupon is good
for 5 eskimo kisses
(rub noses!)

Date:

Special Feelings:

Dear Daddy,
I will color a
picture for the
refrigerator.

Date:

Special Feelings:

Dear Daddy,
This coupon is good
for rainy day
puddle splashing.

Date:

Special Feelings:

Dear Daddy,
I will help you
take the dog
for a walk.

Date:

Special Feelings:

Dear Daddy,
This coupon is
good for a walk
to the park.

Date:

Special Feelings:

Dear Daddy,
I will tell you
what I did at
school today.

Date:

Special Feelings:

Dear Daddy,
I will pat your
back when you
are sick.

Date:

Special Feelings:

Dear Daddy,
I will not
ask you "why"
too many times.

Date:

Special Feelings:

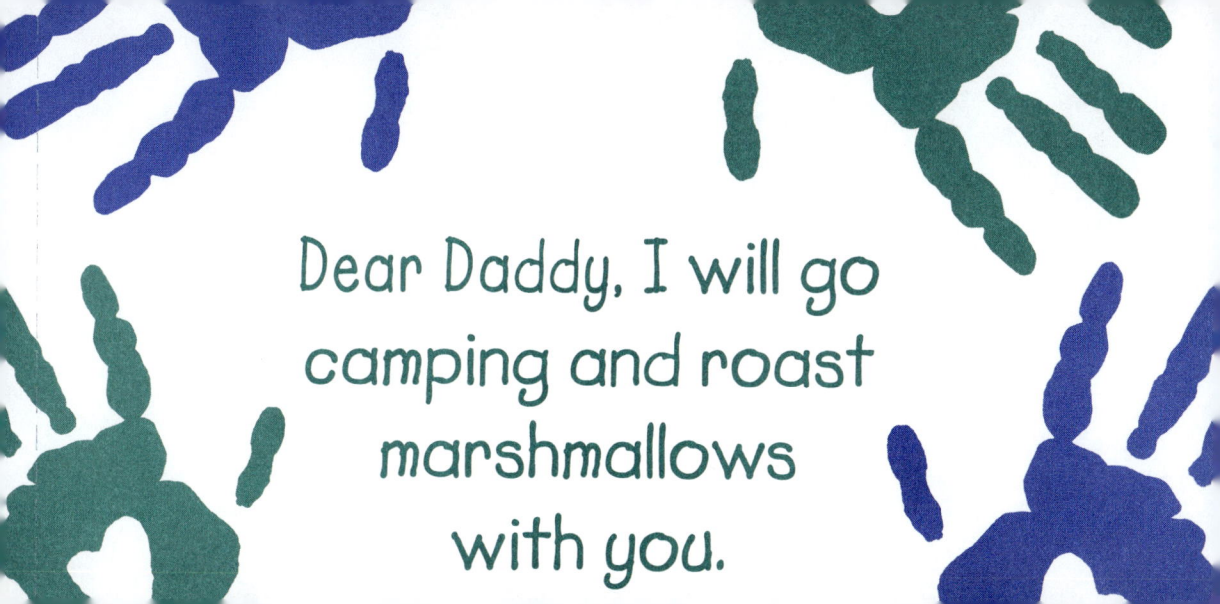

Dear Daddy, I will go camping and roast marshmallows with you.

Date:

Special Feelings:

Dear Daddy,
I will hold
your hand in
the parking lot.

Date:

Special Feelings:

Dear Daddy,
I will let you catch
the biggest fish
when we go fishing.

Date:

Special Feelings:

Dear Daddy,
I will help you play
in the leaves.

Date:

Special Feelings:

Dear Daddy,
I will wipe my feet
before coming
in the house.

Date:

Special Feelings:

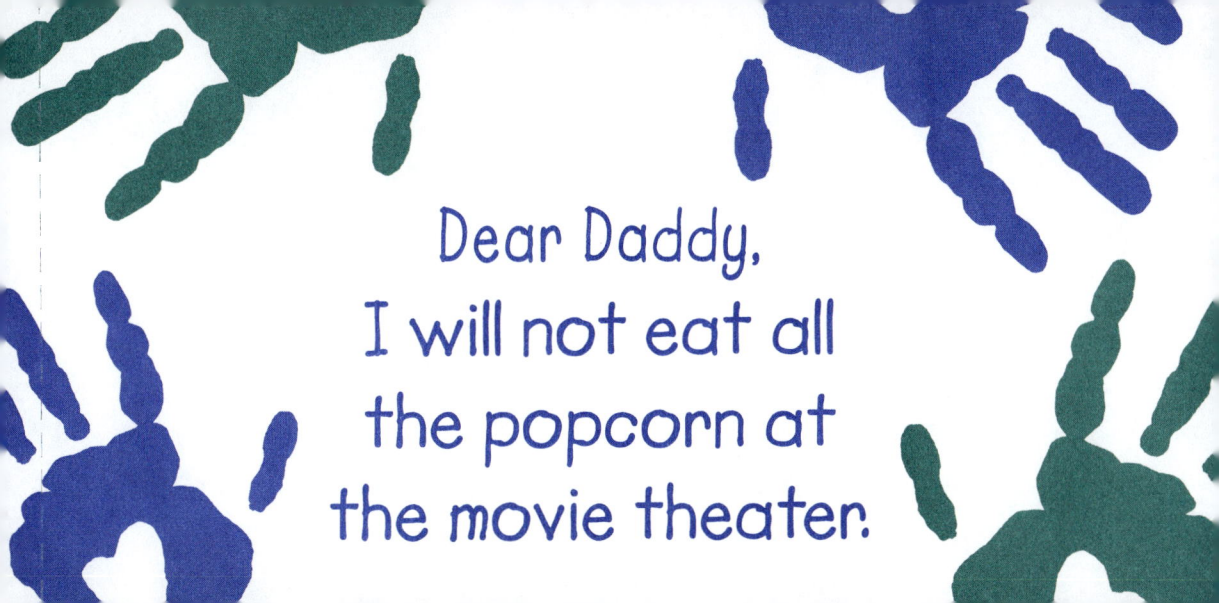

Dear Daddy,
I will not eat all
the popcorn at
the movie theater.

Date:

Special Feelings:

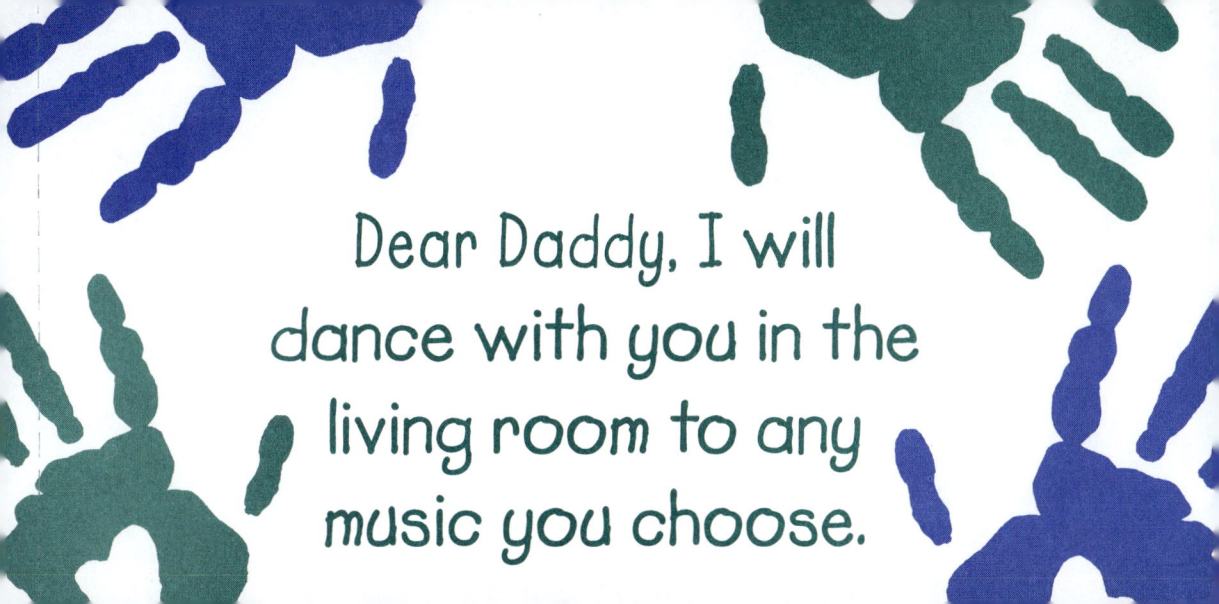

Dear Daddy, I will dance with you in the living room to any music you choose.

Date:

Special Feelings:

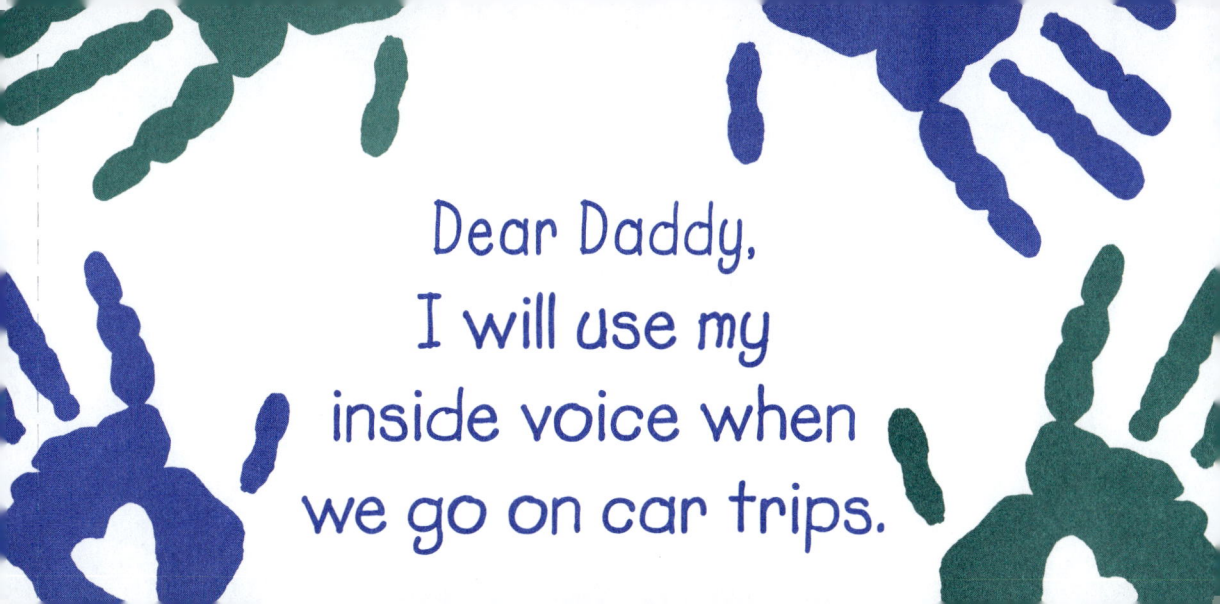

Dear Daddy,
I will use my
inside voice when
we go on car trips.

Date:

Special Feelings:

Dear Daddy,
I will help you
wash your car.

Date:

Special Feelings:

Dear Daddy,
I will clean
my room.

Date:

Special Feelings:

Dear Daddy,
I will wear my mittens
and hat when we
play in the snow.

Date:

Special Feelings:

Dear Daddy, I will use my fork and spoon (and not my hands) at dinnertime.

Date:

Special Feelings:

Dear Daddy,
This coupon
tells me to
"ask Mommy!"

Date:

Special Feelings:

Dear Daddy,
I will keep my seatbelt
on when we are
in the car.

Date:

Special Feelings:

Dear Daddy,
I will play quietly when
you are napping
on the couch.

Date:

Special Feelings:

Dear Daddy,
I will help you keep
the yard clean.

Date:

Special Feelings:

Dear Daddy,
I will let you have one
uninterrupted
phone call.

Date:

Special Feelings:

Dear Daddy,
Tonight, I will share
your favorite
chair with you.

Date:

Special Feelings:

Dear Daddy,
I will share my
dessert with you.

Date:

Special Feelings:

Dear Daddy,
I will let you pick
my bedtime story.

Date:

Special Feelings:

Dear Daddy,
I will dress myself
for school
this morning.

Date:

Special Feelings:

Dear Daddy,
I will eat all
my vegetables.

Date:

Special Feelings:

Dear Daddy,
I will help you
build a treehouse.

Date:

Special Feelings:

Dear Daddy,
I will say
"I love you" each
night before bed.

Date:

Special Feelings:

Send us your coupon idea!

What favors or chores do you do for Daddy to show him your love? Send us your coupon ideas—if we use them in our next book or in future editions, we'll send you a free copy of the finished book! Submission of ideas implies free and clear permission to use in any and all future editions. Send your coupons to:

Sourcebooks, Inc.
Attn: Coupon Ideas
P.O. Box 372
Naperville, IL 60566

Other great coupon books from Sourcebooks

Dear Mommy Coupons
I Love You Mom Coupons
I Love You Dad Coupons
Golf Coupons
The Best of Friends Coupons
The Chocoholic's Coupon Book

Happy Birthday Coupons
My Favorite Teacher Coupons
Merry Christmas Coupons
Love Coupons, by Gregory J.P. Godek,
I Love You Coupons, by Gregory J.P. Godek
author of *10,000 Ways to Say I Love You*

These titles and other Sourcebooks publications are available now at your local book or gift store, or by calling Sourcebooks at 630.961.3900.